DRONE LOGBOOK

ASA-SP-DRONE
ISBN 978-1-61954-998-2

© 2020 Aviation Supplies & Academics, Inc.

Printed in the United States of America

Aviation Supplies & Academics, Inc.
817 Walbridge Street
Kalamazoo, Michigan 49007
Email: asa@asa2fly.com
Website: asa2fly.com

[03]26

Name_____

Mailing Address_____

AF208288

_____

Phone _____ Email_____

Logbook Number_____ From _____ To _____

**Remote Pilot
Certificate Number** _____

Date of Issue _____

YEAR 20___ DATE	UAS MAKE & MODEL	AIRCRAFT ID	LOCATION CITY, LAT/LONG		AIRCRAFT CATEGORY						FLIGHT CONDITIONS				
			FROM	TO	MULTI ROTOR		SINGLE ROTOR		FIXED WING		DAY		NIGHT		ALTITUDE
			PAGE TOTAL												
			AMOUNT FORWARD												
			TOTAL TO DATE												

TYPES OF OPERATING TIME						NUMBER OF FLIGHTS	TO/ LAUNCH	LDG/ RECOVER	TOTAL DURATION OF FLIGHT	REMARKS, MISSION, CREW, WEATHER
DUAL RECEIVED		REMOTE PIC		INSTRUCTOR						
										I certify that the statements made by me on this form are true.
										OPERATOR'S SIGNATURE

| YEAR 20___ DATE | UAS MAKE & MODEL | AIRCRAFT ID | LOCATION CITY, LAT/LONG | | AIRCRAFT CATEGORY | | | | | | FLIGHT CONDITIONS | | | | | |
			FROM	TO	MULTI ROTOR		SINGLE ROTOR		FIXED WING		DAY		NIGHT		ALTITUDE	
			PAGE TOTAL													
			AMOUNT FORWARD													
			TOTAL TO DATE													

TYPES OF OPERATING TIME						NUMBER OF FLIGHTS	TO/ LAUNCH	LDG/ RECOVER	TOTAL DURATION OF FLIGHT	REMARKS, MISSION, CREW, WEATHER
DUAL RECEIVED		REMOTE PIC		INSTRUCTOR						
										I certify that the statements made by me on this form are true.

OPERATOR'S SIGNATURE

| YEAR 20___ DATE | UAS MAKE & MODEL | AIRCRAFT ID | LOCATION CITY, LAT/LONG | | AIRCRAFT CATEGORY | | | | | | FLIGHT CONDITIONS | | | | | |
			FROM	TO	MULTI ROTOR		SINGLE ROTOR		FIXED WING		DAY		NIGHT		ALTITUDE	
PAGE TOTAL																
AMOUNT FORWARD																
TOTAL TO DATE																

TYPES OF OPERATING TIME						NUMBER OF FLIGHTS	TO/ LAUNCH	LDG/ RECOVER	TOTAL DURATION OF FLIGHT	REMARKS, MISSION, CREW, WEATHER
DUAL RECEIVED		REMOTE PIC		INSTRUCTOR						
										I certify that the statements made by me on this form are true.

OPERATOR'S SIGNATURE

YEAR 20___ DATE	UAS MAKE & MODEL	AIRCRAFT ID	LOCATION CITY, LAT/LONG		AIRCRAFT CATEGORY					FLIGHT CONDITIONS					
			FROM	TO	MULTI ROTOR		SINGLE ROTOR		FIXED WING	DAY		NIGHT		ALTITUDE	
PAGE TOTAL															
AMOUNT FORWARD															
TOTAL TO DATE															

TYPES OF OPERATING TIME							NUMBER OF FLIGHTS	TO/ LAUNCH	LDG/ RECOVER	TOTAL DURATION OF FLIGHT	REMARKS, MISSION, CREW, WEATHER
DUAL RECEIVED		REMOTE PIC		INSTRUCTOR							
											I certify that the statements made by me on this form are true.

OPERATOR'S SIGNATURE

GROUND INSTRUCTION LOG

DATE	LESSON PLAN	INSTRUCTOR	TIME	RUNNING TOTAL

GROUND INSTRUCTION LOG

DATE	LESSON PLAN	INSTRUCTOR	TIME	RUNNING TOTAL

MAINTENANCE LOG				
DATE	MAINTENANCE/REPAIR DESCRIPTION	CRASH REPORT	INSPECTION HISTORY	OLD COMPONENT TIME IN SERVICE

MAINTENANCE LOG				
DATE	MAINTENANCE/REPAIR DESCRIPTION	CRASH REPORT	INSPECTION HISTORY	OLD COMPONENT TIME IN SERVICE

UAS FLOWN AND NUMBER OF HOURS IN EACH					
UAS MAKE AND MODEL	PIC	DUAL REC'D	UAS MAKE AND MODEL	PIC	DUAL REC'D

NOTES

Visit **asa2fly.com/uas** for more
remote pilot and drone operator products.

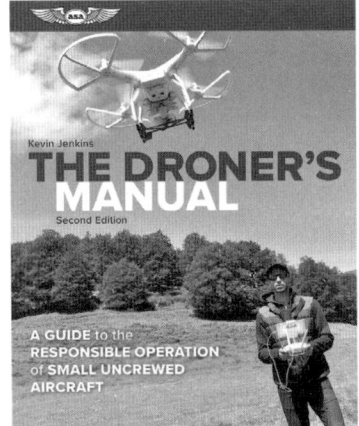

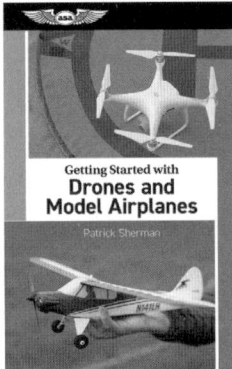

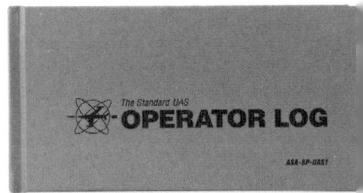